ALL AB

The Brontë Sisters

Carolyn Burns Bass

BLUE RIVER PRESS

Indianapolis, Indiana

Published by Blue River Press
Indianapolis, Indiana
www.brpressbooks.com

Distributed by Cardinal Publishers Group
A Tom Doherty Company, Inc.
www.cardinalpub.com

ISBN: 978-1-68157-088-4

Cover Design: David Miles
Book Design: Rick Korab
Cover Artist: Nicole McCormick Santiago
Editor: Dani McCormick
Illustrator: Colleen Deignan

Printed in the United States of America

10 9 8 7 6 5 4 3 2 1   20 21 22 23 24 25 26 27 28 29

CONTENTS

ALL ABOUT

The Brontë Sisters

Charlotte, Emily, and Anne Brontë were born in northern England in a region known for its dreary, windswept, rocky landscape called the moors. The two eldest Brontë siblings, Maria and Elizabeth, died in childhood, leaving one brother with the three remaining sisters. From their earliest childhood, the Brontë siblings were prolific writers. They wrote about imaginary kingdoms and populated them with villains and heroes.

Charlotte, Emily, and Anne did not marry young as was expected in the early 1800s. Without family money or a husband to support them, they needed to earn their own money. Since they were too educated to be servants, their choices were limited. Their best option was working with children as teachers or governesses. They each taught school or were governesses for a time, but neither Charlotte nor Emily enjoyed teaching. Desperate to find a different way to support themselves, the sisters turned to writing. Knowing it was hard for a woman to succeed in the literary world, they chose male pennames. Charlotte, Emily, and Anne Brontë became Currer, Ellis, and Acton Bell, respectively.

Even using men's names, success didn't come easy. Charlotte's first novel *The Professor* was rejected. Her second novel, *Jane Eyre* was published in 1847. Two months later,

Wuthering Heights by Ellis Bell and *Agnes Grey* by Acton Bell were published. Each of the sisters fought to keep their identity secret. Not even their brother Branwell or their father knew of their publishing success.

Just as the sisters were enjoying the fruit of their creativity, Branwell fell ill with tuberculous and died in September of 1848. Not long afterward, Charlotte lost Emily and Anne to tuberculosis also.

Alone, Charlotte threw herself into her own writing and preserving the legacy of her sisters. In the foreword to a new printing of Emily's *Wuthering Heights*, Charlotte revealed that each of the novels was written by three different sisters. She did not reveal their names, but speculation sparked investigation, which lead to eventual discovery.

Charlotte published two more novels before she married Arthur Bell Nicholls in 1854. Charlotte wrote to her friends how happy she was to be a wife and was overjoyed when she became pregnant in early 1855. Her happiness was cut short by severe morning sickness. Unable to keep down her food and drink, Charlotte became weak and unable to rise from bed. Charlotte died on March 31, 1855 at thirty-eight years old. After her death, Charlotte's husband had her first novel *The Professor* published in 1857.

CHAPTER ONE

The Brontë Family

Charlotte, Emily, and Anne Brontë loved stories even in their early childhood. Their cook and housekeeper, Tabby, often shared spooky stories

Everything but the bell tower of the Haworth church burned down shortly after Reverend Brontë's years. The new church was built above the foundation of the old church with the original clocktower intact.

about growing up among the desolate moors that surrounded the Brontë home.

The Brontë family lived in a home called a parsonage, which was the house provided by the church for their head clergyman to live. The Brontë family moved to the Haworth parsonage in 1820 so that the sisters' father, Reverend Patrick Brontë, could work at St. Michael and All Angels' Church in town. Next door to the parsonage was a very old cemetery with gravestones dating back hundreds of years. All of these elements contributed to the sisters' vivid imaginations.

Charlotte, Emily, and Anne were born five miles away in the small village of Thornton. Charlotte was born April 21, 1816; Emily July 30, 1818; and Anne January 17, 1820. They had three other siblings: Maria, named after their mother and born April 23, 1813; Elizabeth, named after their aunt and born February 8, 1814; and a brother, Branwell, named after their mother's maiden name and born June 26, 1817.

The town of Haworth crept up the side of a hill with a steep cobblestone road leading to the top where the church and parsonage sat. Shops lined each side of the main street leading from the church on the hilltop to the flatland below. Textile mills on the outskirts of town blew smoke into the air day and night, dusting the sky with gloom.

On the edge of town stretched the moors, a type of landscape made of rocky hills with craggy outcroppings and windswept brush. The gritty soil

The town of Haworth sat upon a hill overlooking the rocky moors in the distance.

of the moors was not well suited for crops, though there were many sheep farms in the area. The wind blew hard through the hilltops and valleys of the moors. Few trees survived. Those that did often grew into sinister forms, adding to the eeriness of the landscape.

In the preface to a collection of Emily's poetry, Charlotte wrote:

> The scenery of these hills is not grand; it is not romantic; it is scarcely striking. Long low moors, dark with heath, shut in little valleys, where a stream waters, here and there, a fringe of stunted copse. Mills and scattered cottages chase romance from these valleys; it is only higher up, deep in amongst the ridges of the moors, that Imagination can find rest for the sole of her foot: and even if she finds it there, she must be a solitude-loving raven—no gentle dove. If she demand beauty to inspire her, she must bring it inborn: these moors are too stern to yield any product so delicate.

The Brontë children grew up surrounded by books. Reverend Brontë was educated. He was born in what is now Northern Ireland to a poor farming family with ten children. His Sunday school teacher recognized a thirst for knowledge in the young farmer's son and taught him literature, mathematics,

Reverend Patrick Brontë was the only member of the Brontë family to have had his photograph taken.

Greek, and Latin. As a young man, Reverend Brontë tried to become a blacksmith, a weaver, and a sales person before realizing he wasn't suited to those professions.

Afterward, he became a teacher at several schools in Ireland. In 1802, he applied to St. John's College at England's prestigious Cambridge University and was accepted. He went on to teach at schools in England before settling into a life as a clergyman. He married Maria Branwell in Penzance, Cornwall in 1812.

Sometime during his years in Cambridge he changed the spelling of his family surname from Brunty (sometimes spelled Prunty) to Brontë. He added the two dots upon the "ë" to indicate that the name was pronounced with two syllables. No records exist describing the reason why he changed the surname, though some people think it was to hide his humble Irish beginnings. Others believe he changed it in admiration of Admiral Horatio Nelson, the Duke of Brontë.

In the nineteenth century, poetry was very popular, and people read it aloud to one another as evening entertainment. The Brontë children appeared to have a great fondness for poetry, both in reading it and in writing their own. Their father had published two volumes of poetry before they were born. Reverend Brontë's poetry collections were *Cottage Poems*, published in 1811, and *The Rural Minstrel*,

The Brontë children's aunt moved to Haworth to help raise the children because six children was difficult for Reverend Brontë to manage by himself.

published in 1814. He continued to write poetry throughout his life, while also publishing numerous sermons, pamphlets, and newspaper articles. This rich literary heritage most certainly influenced the Brontë children in their own writings.

Shortly after the Brontë family moved to Haworth, their mother's sister, Aunt Elizabeth Branwell, came to live with them at the parsonage. The Brontë family had six children under the age of eight to care for, and Maria had not regained her health following the birth of baby Anne. The oldest children, Maria and Elizabeth, often helped care for their four younger siblings. They had a very nurturing relationship with one another.

When Anne was only eighteen months old, Mrs. Brontë passed away. Medical science didn't have the technology it has today to understand exactly why she died. The doctor said she had cancer of the uterus, while others said she had a type of childbed fever or infection. Antibiotics had not been invented that could have cured an infection brought on from childbirth.

The Brontë children were devastated by their mother's death. Those who knew their mother recalled her as a lively woman who enjoyed teaching her young children, designing needlework samplers, and reading. Emily and Anne grew up without memories of their mother, but Charlotte often spoke vividly of her in hopes of keeping her memory alive.

Aunt Branwell stayed on with the Brontë family to help Reverend Brontë care for the children and run his household. Although he proposed marriage to several women through the years, none accepted, and he remained a widower for the remainder of his life.

The death of the Brontë children's mother was the first time death touched the family.

CHAPTER TWO

Early Life on the Moors

The small village of Haworth did not have a public school that local children could attend for free. In those days, most education occurred either at home

The moorland surrounding Haworth was windy, rocky and desolate. Emily thought they were the perfect conditions for fertile imaginations to roam freely.

by a parent, tutor, or governess, or at a boarding school by teachers. Reverend Brontë had worked himself from potato-farmer's son to gentleman clergy. He was proud of his success and he wished to see a higher level of achievement for his children.

Most clergymen of Reverend Brontë's level did not earn high salaries so he couldn't afford highly-priced boarding schools. Reverend Brontë taught all of the children the standards of arithmetic, reading, and writing. Although there were no children's books in the house, Reverend Brontë often entertained the children with legends and myths from his childhood in Ireland.

The oldest sister Maria was very precocious in her reading and comprehension. She liked to read aloud to her younger siblings from the newspapers her father brought home. After evening meals, the children often gathered to discuss political or religious topics. The Duke of Wellington, Arthur Wellesley, the Anglo-Irish soldier and statesman who led the defeat of Napoleon Bonaparte in the famous Battle of Waterloo in 1815, was a favorite topic of conversation and debate.

Aunt Branwell taught the girls household tasks such as sewing, needlework, and comportment. They had to learn such things as how to walk, talk, and dress like a lady. The Brontë girls preferred roaming the moors, climbing over the rocks, and following trails up to rocky crags, rather than lessons in comportment, but each of them mastered the ladylike arts as they matured.

Aunt Branwell was a strict teacher, but she was not without love and compassion for her nieces and nephew. When they were not at lessons, the children roamed through the surrounding moorland. Out on the moors, the children played imaginary games of battles and wars, court intrigue, and romance. The Duke of Wellington figured prominently in their pretend lives and would be a major influence in their early writings.

The girls visited a rocky area called Ponden Kirk often. A deserted farmhouse north of Ponden Kirk called Top Withens fascinated the children. They scampered around the ruined structure and imagined stories about the place. In later years, Emily would use the image of this desolate homestead as a model

Ponden Kirk was one of the Brontë children's favorite places to play. Emily describes this rock formation as Penistone Crag in her novel Wuthering Heights.

for the house called Wuthering Heights from which her novel drew its name.

The children often hiked to the stone bridge over South Dean Beck, which descended down the mountain in a waterfall. Near the waterfall was a rock shaped almost like a chair which the children called the stone chair. The waterfall and the stone chair appeared in many of the Brontë's pretend games and later in their writings.

Several years after the death of his wife, Reverend Brontë realized his daughters needed a more challenging education than what he and Aunt Branwell could offer. Reverend Brontë's standing as a clergyman gave him the distinction of gentleman, which would have allowed his children to attend a boarding school for children of gentry. Yet his salary was such that he could not afford tuition at a school for gentleman's daughters. He began researching what was then known as charity schools for the children of distressed families.

In his research, Reverend Brontë discovered that several charity schools in the area had been cited for horrifying mistreatment. Some schools had

Top Withens was hit by lightning in 1893, which caused the damage visitors see today. It tore part of the roof off, blasted holes in the walls, started a fire, and shattered the windows.

A stone bridge spanned South Dean Beck where the Brontë children often played. Today it is the Brontë Bridge.

left serious illnesses untreated, unclean bedrooms with rats gnawing on students in the night, and malnutrition so extreme that students went blind.

At last, Reverend Brontë came upon the Clergy Daughters' School at Cowan Bridge, Lancashire, operated by the Reverend Carus Wilson. It was often referred to simply as Cowan Bridge. The school came with many glowing endorsements from respected people, including the daughter of Hannah Moore, a poet Reverend Brontë recognized. Several of the patrons listed in the pamphlets were strong supporters of education for girls. Best of all, the school tuition was not expensive.

In July of 1824, Maria and Elizabeth were sent to the school at Cowan Bridge. One month later, eight-year-old Charlotte was sent to the same school. Two months after that, Emily, age six, was sent to school with her sisters. Their time at the Clergy Daughters'

The Clergy Daughters' School at Cowan Bridge would later be Charlotte's reference for the school the main character gets sent to in the novel Jane Eyre.

School would forever change the sisters' lives and shape their future literary accomplishments.

The sisters took comfort in being together when they had to go to school. It helped them feel less homesick.

CHAPTER THREE

Tragedy at School

Maria was ten years old and Elizabeth was nine when their father escorted them to Clergy Daughters' School at Cowan Bridge. They were among the youngest students and, being new, were immediately picked on and bullied by the older girls. Relief came shortly thereafter when Charlotte and Emily joined them, but they were even younger than their two older sisters.

Cowan Bridge required all students to wear uniforms. In summer, they wore white frocks on Sundays for church, then yellow frocks during the rest of the week. Throughout the harsh northern winters, the students wore purple frocks made of a heavy woolen material with purple cloaks for additional warmth.

Life at Cowan Bridge was hard. The dormitories were not heated in the winter. Not only was the air extremely cold, but water in their washbasins would often freeze overnight. Each washbasin was shared by six girls, which got dirtier and dirtier after each use. Since there was no indoor plumbing, the girls retreated to an outhouse for their toilet. There was only one outhouse at the school, making for unsanitary conditions for students and staff alike.

During the period the Brontë sisters attended, a typical day at Cowan Bridge started with the girls being woken at dawn by a bell clanging in the

The boarding school dormitories in the 1820s often featured large rooms with rows of beds that would be shared by two children each.

dormitory. The girls were to wash, dress, and be at morning prayers without any assistance from others. Morning prayers began at eight o'clock in the morning and lasted until nine-thirty. After a quick breakfast of porridge, lessons began and went until noon. The students had recess in the school yard until lunch was served.

Lunch commonly consisted of various vegetables, a small slice of meat or cheese, and Yorkshire pudding or bread. After lunch, they were back at lessons until five o'clock when they broke for their late afternoon meal called tea. Tea included of a slice of bread and a cup of coffee, followed by thirty minutes of playtime. Evening lessons went for several hours, finally ending with a supper of oatcake washed down with water or sometimes milk. They gathered for evening prayers, then went to their dormitory for bed.

The headmaster of Cowan Bridge was also the pastor of Tunstall Church. Each week, the girls donned their Sunday frocks and walked, rain or shine, more than three miles to Reverend Wilson's church for services. After church, they were given meager refreshments and then walked back to school for Sunday devotions, lessons on the catechism, and recitation of Bible verses. They had another sermon before bed, then were finally excused to their dormitory.

Charlotte was very small for her age and extremely nearsighted. It got to the point that she had to bring a book directly under her nose to read. She quickly became the subject of bullies who ridiculed her size

Many classrooms at the time were bare and undecorated to limit distractions.

and reading habits. As the youngest student at the school, Emily was resented by many of the students for being a favorite of the teachers.

Growing up in the harsh environment of the Yorkshire moors, the Brontë sisters were accustomed to cold, windy, and stark conditions. Their father was stern and didn't allow fancy clothes or luxurious surroundings like carpets on the cold, flagstone floors. In their Haworth home, the children were not served meat at meal times, but there was enough other healthy vegetables and bread to go around. Even though the Brontë sisters were not used to being pampered, they did not expect the horrible conditions they encountered at Cowan Bridge.

The girls complained among themselves that the breakfast porridge served was either spoiled, burned, or mixed with inedible bits. They were given butter for their bread only on Sundays, and it was often rancid. The meat was stringy, dry, and even spoiled on some occasions.

The teachers were another difficulty for the students. They were rough and demanding, and bullied students in front of other children. The

Brontë sisters, as well as the other students, lived in constant fear of punishment. Schools during the nineteenth century often included physical punishment. Cowan Bridge followed this method, along with other non-physical punishments that were cruel even in their day. Some students were locked in a room without water, food, or recreation for long periods of time. Others were made to sit on a stool for hours without moving.

A fever broke out among the students at Cowan Bridge in early 1825. As girls lay about the dormitories too ill to eat or drink, a doctor was called to check on them. He was outraged by the conditions at the school and insisted that the children be given clean water and nutritious food. He took a bite of meat from the afternoon meal and immediately spit it out, saying it was rotten. Shortly thereafter, the cook was fired. The food quality improved somewhat.

Maria became sick in February of 1825. One morning, she was feeling very weak and having trouble getting dressed for the day when a teacher came in. The teacher grabbed her arm, pulled her up and thrust her into the middle of the room to

Food was meager and unhealthy at the Cowan Bridge school when the Brontë sisters attended.

ridicule her about being slow and sloppy. When she finally appeared at breakfast, she was punished for being late. Maria's health continued to decline. In early May, the school notified Reverend Brontë, who traveled to Cowan Bridge and took Maria home. Maria died at home on May 6, 1825.

Several weeks later, Elizabeth fell sick and was immediately sent home. Charlotte and Emily returned to Haworth for the midsummer holidays in time to see Elizabeth before she died on June 15, 1825. Both of the eldest Brontë sisters died from tuberculosis.

Reverend Brontë, who had already paid the tuition for his daughters, sent Charlotte and Emily back to Cowan Bridge to finish their term. While at school for that session, Charlotte made a new friend in an older girl named Mellaney Hayne, whom she remembered years later. When the summer term was over, Charlotte and Emily returned to a sadder home

Tuberculosis was a very difficult disease at the time that caused bleeding in the lungs. Now, we use antibiotic medication to get rid of it.

in Haworth and clung ever closer to their brother Branwell and their younger sister Anne.

CHAPTER FOUR

Imagination Reigns

Losing two sisters within months was difficult for all of the remaining Brontë children. In later years, Charlotte would recall her year at Cowan Bridge when writing her novel *Jane Eyre*. The main character Jane Eyre is sent as an orphan to a charity school that resembles Cowan Bridge in great detail.

At her fictional school called Lowood, Jane recounts many of the punishments, disgusting food, cruel teachers, and bullying that the Brontë sisters endured at Cowan Bridge. Just as it was at Cowan Bridge, a fever breaks out among the students at the fictional Lowood School. A kind and gentle friend of Jane Eyre's named Helen Burns is humiliated by a teacher during her sickness and later dies, much like Charlotte's sister Maria.

Charlotte, now the eldest, took her older sister's responsibility upon herself and did her best to shepherd her siblings. Lessons with their father and Aunt Branwell resumed. Reverend Brontë also hired John Bradley, a local painter of some renown, as an art teacher. Each of the children enjoyed drawing and painting, often copying pictures from books. The children devoured the great books from their father's study, such as *The Arabian Nights*, *Gulliver's Travels*, and those by Shakespeare. After lessons each day, the children fled to the moors behind their house to play.

The Brontë children loved Tabby so much that when she broke her leg after falling in 1836, the children refused to let her go. They claimed they would look after her as she had looked after them growing up.

With the girls back home, Reverend Brontë realized he needed another hand to help with cooking and housework. Tabby Ackroyd, a woman of around fifty years old, moved into the parsonage to be the cook. She was gruff but encircled the children in a rough kind of love. Tabby had lived her entire life in the desolate moorland and entertained the children with tales of fairies, sprites, ghosts, and other spooky occurrences on the moors. She told them the factories and mills that surrounded the village drove the fairies away from Haworth.

Always full of imagination and ready to act in plays of their own creation, the children began creating fictional worlds based around a set of toy soldiers that their father had brought home to Branwell. Charlotte once wrote the following description of their play acting in a document she called *The History of the Year 1829*:

> Papa bought Branwell some wooden soldiers at Leeds; when Papa came home, it was night, and we were in bed, so next morning Branwell came to our door with a box of soldiers. Emily and I jumped out of bed, and I snatched up one and exclaimed, "This is the Duke of Wellington! This shall be the Duke!" When I had said this, Emily likewise

took one up and said it should be hers; when Anne came down, she said one should be hers. Mine was the prettiest of the whole, and the tallest, and the most perfect in every part. Emily's was a grave-looking fellow, and we called him "Gravey." Anne's was a queer little thing, much like herself, and we called him "Waiting-boy." Branwell chose his, and called him "Bonaparte."

In the years between school at Cowan Bridge and adulthood, the four siblings created imaginary worlds and populated them with intriguing characters, both fictional and real. Intrigued by reading about discoveries and colonization in Africa, the children created an imaginary world on the west coast of Africa called the Glass Town Confederacy. This kingdom was comprised of four territories, each of them controlled by one of the children.

They used Branwell's toy soldiers to imagine elaborate scenes with heroic characters. Some of the characters were modeled after real people, like the Duke of Wellington, and others were made-up, like Gravey. The four children acted as supernatural genies who governed the territories. They drew maps, established a history, waged wars, and wove in political intrigue and romantic plots.

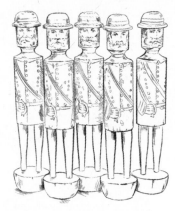

Charlotte and Branwell made miniature books and magazines for the toy soldiers, the pages bound with sewing thread. Inside these tiny books, they wrote histories, poems, and stories in such minuscule printing, most readers need a magnifying glass to read the words. Many of these tiny books still exist in museum collections around the world and some have been digitized and stored online for people to view.

The Brontë children played with a set of wooden soldiers as characters in their imaginary Glass Town Confederacy.

Charlotte and Branwell, being the oldest, were more dominant in the direction of Glass Town and a kingdom they called Angria. Feeling left out, Emily and Anne created a world of their own and called it

Gondal. Emily and Anne were just as detailed with developing the geography, culture, and history of their imaginary island as Charlotte and Branwell.

Unfortunately, the Gondal stories written by Emily and Anne were likely destroyed by Charlotte in an attempt to protect their privacy after their deaths. References to Gondal, as well as poetry written about the kingdom, appear frequently in Emily and Anne's letters and their diary fragments that survive.

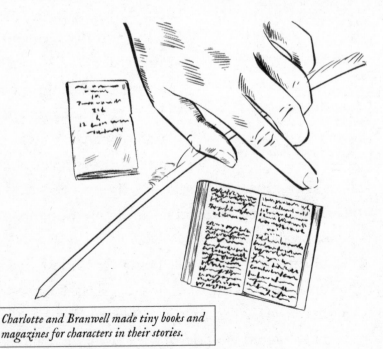

Charlotte and Branwell made tiny books and magazines for characters in their stories.

CHAPTER FIVE

Education and Imagination

When Charlotte was fourteen years old, Reverend Brontë found a new school for her to attend. The plan was for Charlotte to learn everything she could in a year or so, then come home to teach Emily and Anne. Roe Head School was not a charity school and admitted daughters of well-to-do merchants and other professionals.

The school was run by Miss Margaret Wooler and her three sisters in a large house. Reverend Brontë was encouraged by the school's excellent reputation for academics as well as the comfort of the students. Charlotte entered Roe Head School on January 17, 1831.

Even though Roe Head School was not as far away as Cowan Bridge had been, Charlotte was

This image is based off a sketch by Charlotte Brontë that she made sometime while she was at Roe Head School.

very homesick upon arrival. She was still very small, had never grown as tall as Emily, and even her youngest sister Anne had outgrown her. She was very slender, her clothes were old, and with her poor eyesight, many people thought of her as awkward. One of her first friends, Mary Taylor, described her to Charlotte's first biographer, Elizabeth Cleghorn Gaskell, like this:

I first saw her coming out of a covered cart in very old-fashioned clothes and looking very cold and miserable. She was coming to school at Miss Wooler's. When she appeared in the schoolroom, her dress was changed but just as old. She looked a little old woman, so short-sighted that she always appeared to be seeking something and moving her head from side to side to catch a sight of it. She was very shy and nervous and spoke with a strong Irish accent. When a book was given her, she dropped her head over it 'til her nose nearly touched it, and when she was told to hold her head up, up went the book after it, still close to her nose.

Charlotte's life at Miss Wooler's might have started off rocky, but within days she had knit herself into the life of the school. Two girls from Miss Wooler's school would become her lifelong friends. In addition to Mary Taylor, another new girl named Ellen Nussey befriended her. In her lifetime,

Ellen Nussey and Charlotte became friends quickly while at school together. Over the course of their lives, they would exchange more than 600 letters.

Charlotte would write more than 600 letters to Ellen Nussey, all of which Ellen kept. She wrote regularly to Mary Taylor as well, but Mary didn't keep the letters.

At night, the girls lay in their dormitory beds whispering and telling tales. One of the school legends was of a female ghost who roamed the unoccupied third floor attic of the house. The girls would imagine they heard the rustling of her silk skirts or her moaning in pain. Everyone loved Charlotte's stories, for she had a flair for spooky stories. One night, she added a loud scream to her story, which brought Miss Wooler upstairs to check on the girls. One of the girls was shivering with fright.

Miss Wooler was a gentle but thorough teacher. When Miss Wooler first assessed Charlotte's learning level, she recommended Charlotte be placed in the lower class. Upon hearing this, Charlotte broke into tears, melting her teacher's heart so much Miss Wooler moved her to the top class. The girls in the top class were perplexed by Charlotte. On one hand, Charlotte could recite pages of poetry, but didn't understand grammar.

Knowing she was behind in each of the subjects taught in her class, Charlotte buried herself in schoolwork. Because of her poor eyesight, she never

The girls in Charlotte's dormitory laid awake at night imagining sounds of a ghostly woman moving around in the attic of the school.

played sporting games in the schoolyard. Her friend Mary Taylor recalls her standing or sitting by herself, her nose in a book. Before long, Charlotte had earned her place in the top class by mastering the material being taught.

Within eighteen months, Charlotte had completed studies at Roe Head School, aced her examinations and returned home to Haworth in June of 1832 with a certificate of completion.

Lessons had continued for the remaining Brontë children while Charlotte was away at Roe Head School. Reverend Brontë added Greek and Latin to Branwell's lessons, while Aunt Branwell taught French to Emily and Anne.

Once she was home, Charlotte began lessons with Emily and Anne. When the weather was good, they would walk through the moors to the waterfall where they held class. It's not hard to imagine Charlotte sitting in the stone chair, describing how to use punctuation and proper grammar to her two sisters.

While Charlotte was away in Roe Head, Reverend Brontë obtained a grant from the National School Society to build a Sunday school for the town

*Charlotte, Emily, and Anne called this rock the
stone chair and often came here to play or write.*

children. During this period in history, children of
the working class only went to school on Sundays,
if they went at all. Sunday school was not just for
learning Bible stories, but also basic math, the
alphabet, reading, and writing. The Sunday school

The Brontë children wrote about fanastic imaginary kingdoms and all of the adventures and politics that happened there.

building was constructed between the Brontë's home and the church. Each of the Brontë children taught classes in the Sunday school at some time in their life.

Back home again, Charlotte and Branwell resumed writing, illustrating, and publishing their tiny magazines and books for their imagined Angria kingdom. Emily and Anne continued writing about their pretend Gondal kingdom. In one of the Gondal papers known to exist, Emily blended real life events with her imaginary world.

> The Emperors and Empresses of Gondal and Gaaldine preparing to depart from Gaaldine to Gondal to prepare for the coronation which will be on the twelfth July. Queen Vittoria ascended the throne this month.

This image is based off a watercolor portait of Anne that Charlotte painted.

When they were about sixteen and fifteen years old respectfully, Emily and Anne made a pact to write a summary of their lives every four years. They were to hide it away and then open it on Emily's birthday forty years later. The first of Emily's "birthday papers" from 1834 said:

> Anne and I say I wonder what we shall be like, and what we shall be, and where we shall be if all goes on well in the year 1874—in which year I shall be in my fifty-[sixth] year, Anne will be going in her fifty-fifth year, Branwell will be going in his fifty-eighth year, and Charlotte in her fifty-ninth year. Hoping we shall all be well at that time, we close our paper.

Emily would go on to write summaries of her life in the years 1837, 1841, and 1845, while Anne wrote similar summaries in 1841 and 1845.

CHAPTER SIX

Lessons in Life and Living

As the Brontë children grew, so did the concern for their future. The three sisters—who were considered plain, scholarly dreamers—were said to have little hope of finding husbands to provide for them. It wasn't until the latter half of the twentieth century that women worked outside the home because they enjoyed the job.

Until then, it was expected of men to marry and women to have children and manage a household. The only jobs open to educated women at the time when the Brontë sisters lived were positions as teachers or governesses. When women married, they were expected to quit their jobs so they could be wives and mothers.

Reverend Brontë had serious health issues around this time and was developing cataracts in his eyes. His greatest hope was to see his daughters placed as governesses or teachers, and his son set up in a business that could support a family of his own. Plus, in the nineteenth century, a man with unmarried sisters was expected to care for his sisters in their old age. How was Branwell to do all of this, and still be the master of imaginary worlds? Unable to rely on Branwell, Charlotte, Emily, and Anne expected to find their way in the world on their own.

Branwell was considered the most promising of the children, and Reverend Brontë had high hopes for his son. He was said to be very charming and handsome with bright red hair. Reverend Brontë had provided Branwell with private lessons in drawing, piano, flute, and even boxing. Despite these advantages, Branwell didn't have the same determination to rise above his station as his father had in his youth. He had already dismissed the notion of following his father's footsteps into the clergy.

The family had no money to send Branwell to university where he could have studied law, medicine, or business. Although he was well educated in literature and the classics, Branwell wasn't ambitious enough to win university scholarships as his father had. On top of that, he had a terrible temper and used it to get what he wanted from his father and his sisters. The only vocation that seemed to please Branwell was painting.

One of Branwell's early paintings features Charlotte, Emily, and Anne. It is said to have captured the likenesses of the sisters as young girls, even though the painting technique wasn't very good. The painting has a strange, ghost-like pillar in

This image is based off a self-portrait painted by Branwell.

between Anne and Emily. Looking deeply into the pillar, one sees the outline of a man. Experts believe Branwell originally drew himself in, then painted over his unfinished image. No one knows exactly why Branwell painted himself out of the picture.

This painting, now called "The Brontë Sisters," has become the most iconic image of the sisters and hangs in the National Portrait Gallery in London.

In 1835, when he was eighteen years old, Branwell decided he would attend the Royal Academy of Art in London. It wasn't his father's first choice for Branwell, but Reverend Brontë consented. Photography was a very new technology in the mid-nineteenth century. It was limited to black and white or brown and was very expensive. Many people still wanted to have a color painting of themselves or their family. Painters were fairly common in those days, and a good painter could earn a significant income.

The problem was money. In order to help her family succeed, Charlotte had to leave home to become a governess or a teacher. Her earnings would be used to pay tuition for Emily to attend school, so that their father could pay for Branwell to attend the Royal Academy of Art. In July of 1835, Charlotte wrote to her good friend Ellen Nussey saying, "We are all about to divide, break up, separate. Emily is going to school, Branwell is going to London, and I am going to be a governess."

In her jolly way, Charlotte went on to explain to Ellen that, in truth, she was taking a teaching position at Roe Head School. In fact, she had turned down two offers to be a governess in favor of

This is based on the most recognizable image of the Brontë sisters Anne, Emily, and Charlotte painted by their brother Branwell.

teaching alongside her beloved Miss Wooler. On top of that, Emily would accompany Charlotte to Roe Head School as a student.

Charlotte was delighted to be back with Miss Wooler, though she missed her family. During her three years teaching with Miss Wooler, Charlotte's letters to and from Anne helped her feel better.

Charlotte enjoyed teaching and often read aloud to her students.

She always asked for news about Angria, because Branwell continued to plan events and situations in her absence. Once, while sitting before her students in class, she found herself daydreaming about her Angrian hero, the dashing Duke of Zamorna.

This image is based off a portait of Emily that Branwell painted in 1833.

She was a capable teacher, but found her students dull and unimaginative. She had no more patience for schoolgirl drama as a teacher than she did as a student. In her mind, teaching was only a means to an end, and that end was seeing Branwell set up in a profession worthy of the family's hopes for him.

Emily, at seventeen, was one of the oldest girls at Roe Head School. Even though she was there with her sister, Emily was severely homesick and miserable. She made no friends, secluding herself to write poetry and letters to Anne when not in the classroom.

Seeing her sister suffering, Charlotte prevailed upon her father and Miss Wooler to allow Emily to return home. Back at home, Emily's countenance improved and she poured herself into self-driven lessons. So eager to get outdoors for her solitary walks on the moors, she multi-tasked her housework with her studies. It was not unusual for Aunt Branwell to walk into the kitchen to see Emily with a book propped open, eyes poring over a page while her hands kneaded bread dough.

Anne later painted her pet merlin, Nero, in 1841, showing off her observation skills by including details on his feathers and feet.

Emily loved animals and was known to adopt any strays she came across. Once, when she was walking through the moors, she came across an injured merlin, a type of falcon. She brought the falcon home and nursed it back to life. She named the falcon Nero.

Miss Wooler allowed Anne to take Emily's place at Roe Head School in 1835. Fifteen-year-old Anne struggled at Roe Head School but proved to be a determined student. She won a coveted good conduct award from Miss Wooler at the end of her first year. Toward the end of her final term at Roe Head School, Anne fell gravely ill. Always a religious girl, she worried about her salvation should she die.

A clergyman named Reverend James La Trobe was called. He presented to her a merciful God that brought Anne much peace, rather than the vengeful God in Christian teaching at that time. Anne remained the most devout of all the Brontë siblings. Concerned about her ailing sister, no doubt imagining it would be Maria and Elizabeth all over again, Charlotte demanded that Anne be sent home to recover. Anne returned to Haworth in December of 1837.

Over the Christmas holiday break, Charlotte and Branwell—who had never made it to the Royal Academy of Art—buoyed themselves with a plan to have their poetry published. Branwell wrote a very lengthy letter and enclosed a sample of his poetry to the renowned poet William Wordsworth. Branwell entreated Wordsworth to reply whether or not the great man saw worth in his poetry. He never heard back from Wordsworth. Charlotte sent a letter and a poem to Robert

Robert Southey was a very well-known poet at the time, so Charlotte asked his opinion of her writing. Though he dismissed her and her writing, she is now much more famous than he is.

Southey, the poet laureate of Britain. In her letter to Mr. Southey, Charlotte told him she wanted "to be forever known."

Mr. Southey responded to Charlotte with an encouraging, and yet discouraging, letter. Mr. Southey's letter of March 12, 1837, to the woman who in ten years' time would write one of the first feminist novels, the classic *Jane Eyre*, read:

The daydreams in which you habitually indulge are likely to induce a distempered state of mind . . . . Literature cannot be the business of a woman's life, and it not ought to be. The more she is engaged in the proper duties, the less leisure she will have for it, even as an accomplishment and a recreation. To those duties you have not yet been called, and when you are, you will be less eager for celebrity.

The letter from Robert Southey was found folded and creased from Charlotte rereading it over and over, though it was clear it didn't dampen Charlotte's enthusiasm.

Charlotte was initially disappointed, but close examination of the letter after her death shows the letter had been read repeatedly. She responded to Mr. Southey on March 16, 1837, summarizing his response with an optimistic spin:

> You do not forbid me to write; you do not say that what I write is utterly destitute of merit. You only warn me against the folly of neglecting real duties, for the sake of imaginative pleasures.

Charlotte closed her letter to Mr. Southey with, "I trust I shall never more feel ambitious to see my name in print; if the wish should rise, I'll look at [your] letter and suppress it."

Charlotte kept Mr. Southey's letter preserved in a wrapper labeled: "Southey's Advice | To be kept forever."

CHAPTER SEVEN

Romance and Disappointments

When he was almost nineteen years old, Branwell set up an art studio in nearby Bradford and took lodging with a family there. The three sisters had now completed their education and were expected to begin earning a living. In September of 1838, Emily took a post as a teacher at Law Hill School in Halifax, a bustling town about ten miles south of Haworth. Charlotte continued teaching at Roe Head School, but was becoming even more dissatisfied.

Miss Wooler moved her school to a new building in nearby Dewsbury Moor, a location Charlotte found dreary. Many of the poems Charlotte wrote during this time reflect her loneliness and disappointment in life. In December of 1838, Charlotte collapsed from what would today be considered severe anxiety and depression.

She was sent home to the parsonage and put to solitary bed rest for several days. Her friends Mary and Martha Taylor came to visit and helped cheer up Charlotte during her illness. After a couple of weeks, Charlotte had recovered, but gave up her teaching position with Miss Wooler. At home in the parsonage, she began writing stories for her Angria characters once again.

Each of the sisters was considered plain and old-fashioned in appearance. Despite being the educated daughters of a respected vicar, men didn't

Emily was a teacher at Law Hill School in Halifax.

seem interested in them. It came as quite a surprise to Charlotte when the brother of her friend Ellen Nussey sent her a letter asking her to be his wife. She had met him on several occasions when she had visited Ellen at the Nussey home and, though she found him cordial, was not drawn to him.

The letter did not say that he was in love with her, only that he had become a clergyman and was in need of a wife who could help teach Sunday School in his parish. This kind of marriage proposal did not impress the romantic-natured Charlotte. An excerpt of the letter she returned to him on March 5, 1839 read:

> I am not the serious, grave, cool-headed
> individual you suppose; you would think
> me romantic and eccentric; you would
> say I was satirical and severe. However, I
> scorn deceit, and I will never, for the sake
> of attaining the distinction of matrimony
> and escaping the stigma of an old maid,
> take a worthy man whom I am conscious
> I cannot render happy.

Charlotte would recall this pragmatic proposal several years later in writing *Jane Eyre*. Her title character, Jane, turns down the serious St. John Rivers, who wants a wife only to fulfill his needs as a Christian missionary.

This image is base off a portrait of Charlotte that was commissioned by her publisher. It was painted by a notable artist of the time, George Richmond.

Emily's position at Law Hill School required seventeen-hour work days. Like Charlotte, she did not enjoy being a teacher. She didn't have time to write her Gondal stories, and she missed her family and walks on the moors. In April of 1839, she became seriously ill again and returned to Haworth. Emily never held another job, though she did take on a greater role in housekeeping at the parsonage.

With Charlotte and Emily at home recovering from their illnesses, in May of 1839, Anne took a position as governess with the Ingham family of nearby Blake Hall at Mirfield. Anne was to prepare four of the five young Ingham children for boarding school. The oldest child was a six-year-old boy, and the youngest was a two-year-old girl. Two children were between them in age. There was also a baby, but Anne was not charged with her care.

The children were undisciplined and spoiled, without any interest in learning even the basics of the alphabet and numbers. After nine months without progress, she was dismissed and sent home

Anne's first governess position was at Blake Hall in Mirfield.

to Haworth. Anne would later draw upon her experience as governess at Blake Hall in her classic novel, *Agnes Grey*.

Five months later, Anne was offered another governess position, this time for the Robinson family of Thorp Green Hall. The Robinson children were older than her previous charges and not as unruly. At first, Anne was shy and uncomfortable at the large country house, but her employers were kind and understanding. She soon learned to appreciate her new position and stayed with the Robinson family for five years.

Each summer, the Robinsons took Anne with them on a five-week vacation to the seaside town of Scarborough. Anne fell in love with the sea and counted her time in Scarbrorough as among the happiest in her life. Those who knew the Scarborough area at the time saw similarities between the final setting in Anne's *Agnes Grey*, as well as in her second novel, *The Tenant of Wildfell Hall*.

Branwell had, by this time, failed at becoming a painter. He was dismissed from a job as tutor for a couple of boys, and was fired from his job as a railroad shipping clerk. When a tutor was needed at Thorp Green Hall, Anne convinced the Robinsons to hire Branwell. She would later regret the introduction of her brother into the Robinson home when she realized Branwell was in love with Mrs. Robinson.

In June 1845, Anne resigned her position at Thorp Green Hall, despite the Robinsons' protests. However, one month later, Branwell was dismissed in disgrace after his affair with

Anne was governess for the Robinson children of Thorp Green Hall for five years.

Mrs. Robinson was discovered. Brontë scholars believe Anne left in humiliation from knowing of Branwell's deceitful behavior.

After Charlotte had recovered her health and spirits, she took a position as governess to the Sidgwick family in a small town called Stonegappe, about eight miles north of Haworth. Charlotte found her charges just as unruly as Anne's had been. One of the boys even threw a Bible at Charlotte during lessons. This incident is later recounted in her novel *Jane Eyre* when a character named John Reed throws a book at the young Jane. Charlotte's employment with the Sidgwicks lasted just a few months, then she was back home at the parsonage.

Upon her return from Stonegappe, Charlotte received another marriage proposal. A young Irish curate named Mr. Bryce had come to visit the parsonage with his vicar, who had once been the curate for Reverend Brontë. He was so enamored by Charlotte's wit and vitality, he proposed in a letter to Charlotte only a few days after meeting her. She turned him down. She wrote to Ellen Nussey that he was lively but lacked the fine manners of an Englishman.

Charlotte took one more position as a governess in 1841, which lasted about eight months before she quit and returned to the parsonage with a new idea. She would recruit her sisters to start a school for young ladies right there in Haworth.

Charlotte, Emily, and Anne by now had the qualifications to operate a school, but felt their French could use some field study to perfect it. In February of 1842, Charlotte and Emily left for school in Brussels, a city in Belgium where French is the native language. They enrolled in Pensionnat Héger,

Charlotte was a governess at Stonegappe, the home of the Sidgwick family.

a boarding school where Charlotte would teach English and Emily would teach music in exchange for their tuition and food.

Constantin Héger was schoolmaster of the Pensionnat Héger in Brussels where Charlotte and Emily studied French.

Charlotte thrived in the new situation, but Emily never felt comfortable. When their Aunt Branwell died in October of that year, Charlotte and Emily returned to the parsonage. The sisters were astonished to learn that Aunt Branwell left each of them a legacy of £300, which is about $12,000 now.

With the money from Aunt Branwell, the ability to start a school was closer than ever. The timing, however wasn't yet right. Charlotte believed she needed more time learning French before starting the school. Plus, she had developed a very close relationship to the school's headmaster, Constantin Héger. Emily was so glad to be back home, that she didn't want to return to Brussels. Emily stepped into Aunt Branwell's position of managing the parsonage for her father.

Charlotte returned to Brussels and continued teaching English and studying French at Pensionnat Héger for one more year. Her admiration for headmaster Héger grew more visible, straining her relationship with his wife, who also taught at the school. Charlotte realized she needed to leave the pensionnat and Héger. She returned to Haworth on January 1, 1844, leaving behind a man who many believe was inspiration for Mr. Rochester in *Jane Eyre*, as well as William Crimsworth in *The Professor*, both love interests of the main characters.

Upon her return to England, Charlotte resumed plans with Emily and Anne about starting their own school. In July of 1844, Charlotte had an advertisement printed which said:

THE MISSES BRONTË'S ESTABLISHMENT
FOR
THE BOARD AND EDUCATION
OF A LIMITED NUMBER OF
YOUNG LADIES,
THE PARSONAGE, HAWORTH,
NEAR BRADFORD.

In October of that same year, the sisters abandoned the idea of their own boarding school for girls when no one applied for admission.

CHAPTER EIGHT

Writing to be Read

Aunt Branwell's legacy to the sisters relieved their immediate need to find jobs to support themselves. Branwell likely used his aunt's legacy to pay his debts and to drink at the Black Bull pub just down the lane from the parsonage. Although he had a couple of poems published, Branwell had never found success in any kind of work and spent most his days sick from drinking alcohol the previous night. He often came home drunk and woke the family with outbursts of love for Lydia Robinson, his employer's wife from Thorp Green Hall.

Branwell disappointed his father and sisters, but they still loved him. As long as Reverend Brontë was able to continue his work as vicar of the parish, they were guaranteed a home in the parsonage. Still, their father was getting on in years and was nearly blind

Branwell and Lydia Robinson had a romantic relationship that wasn't allowed and caused Anne to resign her position out of shame.

by cataracts in his eyes. The sisters knew that once their father retired or died, they could not count on Branwell to support them, and their aunt's legacy was not enough to live by.

Having been separated for so long by jobs, the sisters no longer read their work to each other or shared their writing as they once had. Emily and Anne still wrote stories based in their Gondal kingdoms, but had also begun writing stories set in the real world. Charlotte had abandoned her Angria kingdom, but sometimes wrote of her Angria characters living in the Yorkshire region. Each of the sisters had started writing novels the other sisters didn't know about.

Early in 1846, Charlotte discovered a notebook into which Emily had copied a collection of her poems. Charlotte was astonished by the beauty and passion of Emily's poetry and believed they were worthy of publishing. Charlotte later wrote this about Emily's poetry, "To my ear, they had also a peculiar music—wild, melancholy, and elevating." She also wrote, "no woman that ever lived—ever wrote such poetry before."

When Charlotte approached Emily with the notebook, Emily blew into a furious rage at having her privacy invaded. It took a couple of days before Charlotte and Anne calmed her down enough to consider sending the poetry to a publisher. Charlotte and Anne suggested they combine the best of their poetry with Emily's and submit them as one collection written by three people. Emily insisted that they should not use their real names. Charlotte, who knew the publishing world better than her sisters, agreed.

The publishing world in those days was a world for men. Very few women had found success in poetry or novel writing. When they did, their work was not judged for its merit alone, but in light of it being written by a woman. Charlotte wanted their poetry to be judged for its quality, not because it was written by women.

The sisters chose pseudonyms which were typically masculine names, each keeping their own initials. Charlotte would be Currer Bell, Emily would be Ellis Bell, and Anne would be Acton Bell. They all agreed: no one would know of their true identities. Not their father, and especially not Branwell. When he was drinking at the pub, Branwell would talk about anything. He couldn't be trusted to keep a secret.

Charlotte began writing letters to publishers asking them to accept their poems. None of those she contacted were interested in a collection of poetry by three unknown writers. Charlotte reached out to a periodical for advice and was directed to a publisher in London known as Aylott and Jones. After much writing back and forth, Aylott and Jones agreed to publish the Bell poetry collection at the author's expense.

The sisters pooled their resources and paid to publish 1,000 copies of *Poems by Currer, Ellis and Acton Bell*. When the book was published in May of 1846, it received three positive reviews from critics who had received free copies. The collection, however, only sold two copies.

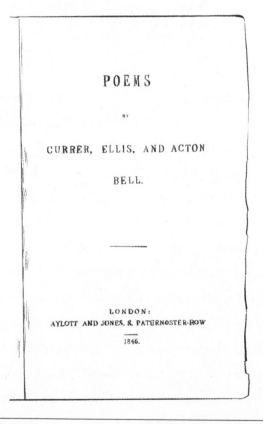

POEMS

BY

CURRER, ELLIS, AND ACTON

BELL.

LONDON:
AYLOTT AND JONES, & PATERNOSTER-ROW

1846.

The Brontës chose male names to originally publish under because they thought it would increase their chances of being published.

CHAPTER NINE

Publishing Success

The dismal sales of the sisters' poetry collection disappointed the sisters. They did not give up, though. They learned that more money could be made by publishing novels. Each of the sisters had much experience writing fiction and already had novels underway. They went directly to work polishing their novels for submission to publishers.

Charlotte had written a novel called *The Professor* about a school master who falls in love with one of his students. Emily had been working on a novel called *Wuthering Heights* set right there in the gloomy moors. It was the doomed love story of a woman named Catherine and her soul-mate named Heathcliff who grew up as adopted brother and sister. Anne had previously written a novel about the stages of a young woman's life. Anne began revising the novel, renaming it *Agnes Grey*.

The sisters resumed their former routines of writing furiously in the dining room of the parsonage until nine o'clock in the evening. Once they put away their writing material, they would pace about the room, circling the dining room table, discussing

The dining room of the parsonage where the Brontë sisters wrote their books.

their work. The stationer in Haworth later recalled how the sisters came into his shop frequently during this time to buy paper.

In early 1847, the sisters began sending to publishers a package containing three novel manuscripts: *Wuthering Heights* by Ellis Bell, *Agnes Grey* by Acton Bell, and *The Professor* by Currer Bell. The manuscripts were rejected many times, and the package returned. Each time the package of manuscripts was delivered back to the parsonage, Charlotte would apply a new publisher's mailing label and send it out again.

Finally, in July of that year, the publishing house of Thomas Cautley Newby sent Charlotte a letter. They wanted to publish *Wuthering Heights* and *Agnes Grey*, but not *The Professor*. Charlotte was disappointed, but not discouraged. Emily and Anne were reluctant to be published without Charlotte, but she encouraged them to continue. While *Wuthering Heights* and *Agnes Grey* were being prepared for publishing, Charlotte sent out her new novel manuscript, *Jane Eyre*.

Jane Eyre was snapped up by the publisher Smith, Elder & Company in London. The book was printed

The famous Temple of Muses bookstore on Finsbury Square in London was very likely one of the shops that sold the sisters' books.

without delay and was in bookshops by October 19 of 1847—even before Emily and Anne's novels. *Jane Eyre* was an instant success with critics and readers. Everyone wanted to know more about the exciting new author named Currer Bell.

Despite the pseudonym, critics were abuzz over whether Currer Bell was a man or a woman. One reviewer wrote that the book had to be written by a woman or an upholsterer, for who else would know the precise steps to sewing curtain hooks into the drapery? Still, reviews were overall positive. A critic from the popular magazine called the *Atlas* wrote:

> This is not merely a work of great promise; it is one of absolute performance. It is one of the most powerful domestic romances which have been published for many years. It has little or nothing of the old conventional stamp upon it; none of the jaded, exhausted attributes of a worn-out vein of imagination.

Two months after *Jane Eyre* was published, Emily and Anne's novels were released as a set of three books. *Wuthering Heights* comprised volumes one and two, and *Agnes Grey* was volume three. *Agnes Grey*, a quiet book in comparison to its bold companion, *Wuthering Heights*, was largely overlooked. Those critics who did review *Agnes Grey* found it well written and compelling but compared it unfavorably to *Jane Eyre*.

Wuthering Heights, however, received brutal reviews. Critics mostly agreed that the story was crude and violent, but the writing was remarkable. A critic from *The Spectator* wrote:

Early collectors of the Brontës' books believed that they were written all by the same person, which helped make the books more popular as people tried to solve the mystery of the authors' identities.

the incidents are too coarse and disagreeable to be attractive, the very best being improbable, with a moral taint about them, and the villainy not leading to results sufficient to justify the elaborate pains taken in depicting it.

The shocking plots and controversial topics within *Jane Eyre* and *Wuthering Heights* fed the public's conjecture that the three Bell books were written by the same person using different names. This was helped along by the unscrupulous publisher of *Wuthering Heights*, Thomas Cautley Newby, who wanted to cash in on the popularity of *Jane Eyre*.

It had always been Branwell's aspiration to publish books, and the sisters didn't want to humiliate him with knowledge of their success.

The sisters were very nervous about letting their father read their work, but Charlotte finally gave her father a copy of Jane Eyre. *Revered Brontë didn't say much, but it was later noted by the family that he was very proud of his daughters' accomplishments.*

Branwell had sunk so far into alcoholism and opium addiction by this time that he could barely hold a pen steady in his hand. Plus, he had become very sick. Everyone was worried for Branwell, especially Reverend Brontë. The sisters decided it would console their father if he knew they had created a good income for themselves.

Charlotte told her father first. She brought in a set of the three volumes of *Jane Eyre* books and told him that she had written a novel. Apparently he was working on something he thought important

Branwell painted himself with his sisters in a setting called "The Gun Group."

because he responded as if he couldn't be bothered. Charlotte pressed on, reading him some of the glowing reviews. This perked his interest, so she left him the volumes to read. Later that afternoon he joined the sisters at tea with enthusiastic praise for *Jane Eyre*. Charlotte then told him that Emily and Anne had also published novels soon to be released. It's not hard to imagine how pleased and proud he was of his daughters.

CHAPTER TEN

A Literary Journey

Money was flowing into the parsonage now, mostly through Charlotte's *Jane Eyre* royalties. The name Currer Bell was becoming widely known in literary circles throughout the English-speaking world. The novel had been printed in America where it had become the most talked-about novel of the season.

Each of the sisters had started writing new novels, but Anne finished first. She sent *The Tenant of Wildfell Hall* to Thomas Newby to be published. A short while later Charlotte received a disturbing letter from her publisher, George Smith, asking why she was selling her new novel, *The Tenant of Wildfell Hall*, to a different publisher—one in America! Charlotte was furious. The dishonorable Newby intended to grab some of the Currer Bell glory by claiming *The*

Tenant of Wildfell Hall was written by the same author as *Jane Eyre*.

Charlotte gathered her sisters together and insisted they go to London to prove to her publisher that the Bells were, indeed, three different people. Anne was upset at Newby, too. After all, it was her creative imagination and hard work that produced *The Tenant of Wildfell Hall*. Why should the credit go to Charlotte? Emily, however, refused to go with them to London. She made them promise they would not reveal her name as author of *Wuthering Heights*.

Charlotte and Anne took the night train to London on July 6, 1848 and showed up at the business address of Smith, Elder & Company. The clerk was reluctant when the two women dressed in country clothing demanded to speak with George Smith. After much insistence, George Smith finally appeared. He scoffed when Charlotte first told him she was Currer Bell, the author of *Jane Eyre*. Only after she produced the letter he had sent to her address did he accept the fact that the petite woman with the Irish accent was his brilliant star author.

He immediately sent for his colleague, William Smith Williams, who had first read the potent manuscript and passed it to George Smith. The meeting then turned into a fan-session, as the two men praised the two sisters. Mr. Smith and Mr. Williams urged Charlotte and Anne to stay a few days so they could introduce them to London's literary society. The sisters agreed, providing Smith and Williams would keep their identities secret. Over the next few days, Charlotte and Anne were introduced as Smith's country cousins, the Brown sisters.

When the sisters visited London, they visited St. Stephen's Church and marveled at the art and architecture.

Those two days were among the most memorable in the sisters' lives. They were taken to the Royal Opera, to worship at St. Stephen's Church, to luncheons, dinners, parks, art galleries, and shopping. All without revealing their real names to anyone except Smith and Williams.

CHAPTER ELEVEN

Final Farewells

Branwell, the beloved brother of Charlotte, Emily, and Anne, never knew of his sisters' success as novelists. Throughout 1848, as the sisters were enjoying the success of their literary labors, Branwell was slipping toward his death. He spent his days sleeping and his nights drinking at the nearby Black Bull pub. He'd become mean and unruly, yelling and bullying his father and sisters. He often came home so drunk that one of the sisters had to help him up the stairs and into his bedroom. One night, he knocked a candle over and set fire to his bed. The sisters smelled the smoke and rushed in with buckets of water to extinguish the fire.

In the summer of 1848, the effects of tuberculosis overtook Branwell's unhealthy lifestyle. As the sisters nursed him, they hoped and prayed for the best, but expected the worst. They had seen these same symptoms in their sisters Maria and Elizabeth before they had died. On September 24, Branwell insisted the sisters help him from bed. He wanted to die standing as a man, not lying in bed as an invalid. After his death, the sisters found his pockets filled with letters from Mrs. Robinson, the married woman from Thorp Green Hall who had broken Branwell's heart.

Branwell's death at age thirty-one shook the sisters hard. Even though he had been difficult to live with through the last few years, the sisters loved him. Charlotte wrote this about Branwell's death in a letter to her friend Ellen Nussey, "'Til the last hour comes, we never know how much we forgive, pity, regret a near relative."

Branwell was buried a week after his death in the family vault beneath the flagstone slabs inside the church of St. Michael and All Angels in Haworth. His mother, his sisters Maria and Elizabeth, and his aunt Elizabeth Branwell lay in graves beside him.

Emily caught a cold at Branwell's funeral. Charlotte and Anne became very concerned because Emily would not even go out on her walks to the moors. As the cold worsened, Charlotte wanted to call for a doctor. Emily refused to be seen or to take medication. Charlotte tried to cheer her up searching the cold moors for a lingering bud of the heather which Emily loved so much. Unfortunately by that time, Emily was so ill she did not recognize the flower or the loving gesture of her sister.

On December 19, like her brother Branwell, she rose from her sickbed, dressed herself, and tried to go about the business of a normal day. She had lost a lot of weight, her complexion was pale, and her breathing was labored. After several hours, she looked to Charlotte and told her she would now see a doctor. By that time, it was too late, the tuberculosis was too far advanced. Emily died at two o'clock that same afternoon at age thirty.

Charlotte and Anne were devastated. They had buried their brother only three months ago and now they had lost their beloved sister. Plus, Charlotte was suspicious of Anne's health failing. Anne had been complaining of a pain in the side and shortness of breath similar to Emily.

As the family walked with the coffin to the church, Emily's massive dog, Keeper, followed behind the

Emily painted this portrait of her dog Keeper, who was said to have followed her coffin into the church during her funeral service.

coffin and into the church. Keeper stayed beside the coffin during the funeral service and burial, then followed the family back home. He slept beside Emily's bedroom door and grieved along with the rest of the family.

Just as Charlotte suspected, the pain in Anne's side progressed into an illness much like Emily's. Anne, however, was eager to see a doctor and accepted treatment without complaint. Her new novel, *The Tenant of Wildfell Hall*, had been published in June of that year—only weeks after Emily's death.

In January, the doctor confirmed that Anne had an advanced case of tuberculosis. As the cold, bitter Yorkshire winter progressed, Anne continued to fight the disease. Anne's doctor suggested Anne might be more comfortable in a warmer climate. Anne, who had fallen in love with the ocean and the coastal town of Scarborough, was elated when the doctor approved her choice. She said tearful goodbyes to her father and the faithful parsonage servants on May 24, 1849.

Ellen Nussey joined Charlotte with Anne on the journey to Scarborough. The three women spent the night in York, where Charlotte and Ellen took Anne sight-seeing in a wheelchair and shopped in

Scarborough was a popular beachside town and many people visited for the nice climate and healthy atmosphere.

the bustling city. The next day, they boarded a train to Scarborough. Anne was determined to enjoy what time she had left in Scarborough. They bought season tickets to the spa where they could swim and stroll along the cliff bridge.

Anne is buried in Scarborough by the sea, not with her sisters in Haworth. Her original headstone mistakenly said she was twenty-eight when she died instead of twenty-nine. It has been corrected, though.

Despite her illness, Anne was determined to revisit the activities she had enjoyed so much during her many visits to Scarborough with the Robinsons. Anne hired a donkey cart and driver for sightseeing along the South Sands of the beach to enjoy the air and insisted upon taking the reins. By the next day, however, Anne began to feel the heaviness of her illness. Charlotte called for a doctor. Anne begged the doctor to tell her the truth of how long she had left, for she wanted to return home.

The doctor doubted that Anne had time to return to her home in Haworth. The next day, May 28, Anne rose and dressed herself just as her sister and brother had done. She settled herself in an easy chair and rested with Charlotte and Ellen nearby. Seeing the grief upon Charlotte, her final words were, "Take courage Charlotte. Take courage." She was only twenty-nine years old.

Rather than have Anne's body shipped home to Haworth, and since she had expressed no preference, Anne was buried beneath the castle wall in St. Mary's Churchyard. Today her grave bears a marker noting her as "Poet and Author."

CHAPTER TWELVE

The End of a Literary Family

Charlotte returned to Haworth with a broken heart and a near-empty home. Only her father remained of the once vibrant family that filled the parsonage. She took comfort in her Christian faith and expressed it in her letters, poems, and writings.

Already working on a new novel called *Shirley* when her sisters died, it featured two young women, Shirley and Caroline. *Shirley* dealt with human rights during the time before England had laws to protect mill and factory workers. Charlotte said she created the character of the spirited *Shirley* by imagining what her sister Emily would have been like if she had been born wealthy. *Shirley* was published October 26, 1849.

Charlotte had maintained her Currer Bell pseudonym with Shirley. Shortly after it was published, an astute reader began to place some of the names, places, and dialects used in Shirley to the town in which he grew up: Haworth.

Knowing the widespread illiteracy of the town, he suspected the only people able to write novels were the parson's children, Charlotte being the only child remaining. He published his suspicion in a Liverpool newspaper, and it spread like wildfire. When Charlotte visited her publisher in London in November, it became harder to maintain her privacy.

That second trip to London in November, nearly a year after Emily's death, was a welcome distraction from the loneliness of the parsonage. Before leaving, she visited a dressmaker and had several new dresses made. She was to stay with Mr. Smith and his family, though she was adamant that she would not be openly introduced as the author of *Jane Eyre* and *Shirley*.

Upon returning to the Smith home after a day of shopping, she was startled to find the renowned author William Makepeace Thackeray waiting for an introduction. Mr. Thackeray was the author of the novel *Vanity Fair*, which had been published around the same time as *Jane Eyre*. When Mr. Thackeray made a comment about cigars that referred directly to *Jane Eyre*, Charlotte knew her cover was blown. She slowly began revealing herself to certain people from that point onward.

Within months of her return home, people throughout England knew the brilliant author of *Jane Eyre* was an ordinary clergyman's daughter in musty old Haworth. Soon people were dropping into church and bribing the sexton to point out the author. She began to be invited to social events among the few families of gentry in the region. Letters from readers were delivered to her at the parsonage. She took great pleasure, and yet found it a duty to respond to her readers. Nevertheless, she continued to use the name of Currer Bell, still striving for her work to be taken on its own merit.

When the critic G. H. Lewes made remarks about the author of *Shirley* being a woman, Charlotte was infuriated. She wrote to him on January 19, 1850 in the name of Currer Bell that said:

Writing after the deaths of her sisters was extremely lonely for Charlotte. She missed being able to discuss plots and characters with them.

I wished critics would judge me as an AUTHOR, not as a woman, you so roughly—I even thought cruelly—handled the question of sex. I dare say you meant no harm, and perhaps you will now be able to understand why I was so grieved at what you will probably deem such a trifle; but grieved I was, and indignant too.

While in London in June of 1850, Charlotte was thrilled to see her childhood idol and hero of her adolescent writings, the Duke of Wellington. He was an old man by then, but still grand in his stature and sparkling uniform. She was impressed enough to write an account of her sighting in a letter to a friend.

Later that summer, Charlotte met another female author who would become a good friend through the rest of her life, Elizabeth Gaskell. Mrs. Gaskell, who would one day write the first biography of her good friend Charlotte Brontë, wrote this observation about Charlotte in a letter to a friend:

> [She is] thin, and more than a half a head shorter than I am; soft brown hair, not very dark; eyes (very good and expressive, looking straight and open at you) of the same color as her hair; a large mouth; the forehead square, broad and rather overhanging. She has a very sweet voice; rather hesitates in choosing her expressions, but when chosen they seem without an effort admirable, and just

befitting the occasion; there is nothing overstrained, but perfectly simple.

The two authors spent several days enjoying the sights of Westmorland in the Lake Country of northwestern England. Charlotte was perfectly comfortable talking about writing, art, and politics with Mrs. Gaskell, but once they joined others, Charlotte was shy. As the year wore on, Charlotte read accounts of herself as written by the hand of social gossips who portrayed her as both a hero and a villain.

Author Elizabeth Gaskell became a good friend of Charlotte. She wrote the first Charlotte Brontë biography after Charlotte's death.

This was the treatment she and her sisters had wanted to avoid when they agreed to publish their work using pseudonyms. Emily and Anne may have died, but their pseudonyms lived. When Smith, Elder & Company approached Charlotte about republishing her dead sisters' books,

Charlotte set to work editing *Wuthering Heights* and *Agnes Grey*.

In December of 1850, the second edition of the two classic novels was published with a very personal foreword written by Charlotte, revealing the novels to be written by her sisters Emily and Anne. The foreword, however, is signed Currer Bell. Although eager to see Anne's *Agnes Grey* republished, she declined to reissue Anne's *The Tenant of Wildfell Hall*. Writing to her publisher's colleague, William Smith Williams, on her reasons for refusal, Charlotte said:

> It had faults of execution, faults of art, was obvious, but faults of intention of feeling could be suspected by none who knew the writer. For my part, I consider the subject unfortunately chosen—it was one the author was not qualified to handle at once vigorously and truthfully.

Charlotte continued traveling throughout the country, attending literary events, lectures, and accepting invitations from her new friends. Her travels were often planned around the health of her father. She continued to write and, in

1853, her third novel *Villette* was published. In *Villette*, Charlotte had drawn widely from her first unpublished novel, *The Professor*, which had been turned down by every publisher. *Villette* received widespread acclaim, cementing Charlotte's career as a writer.

During the years following the death of her brother and sisters, Charlotte had developed a

Charlotte was only married to Arthur Bell Nicholls for a little more than a year before her death.

relationship with her father's curate, Arthur Bell Nicholls. He had fallen in love with Charlotte and, in early 1853, proposed marriage to her. She turned down his proposal at the request of her father, who objected to the marriage because he needed Charlotte to care for him in his failing health. Mr. Nicholls didn't give up, though. He proposed again in January of 1854, and by this time, Charlotte felt enough love for him to accept.

Reverend Brontë was not pleased, thinking a curate was not good enough for his remaining daughter. Charlotte wed Arthur on June 29, 1854 at thirty-eight years old. The couple took a honeymoon to Ireland, then returned to the parsonage where Charlotte found a happiness she had never before known. She started a new novel and continued writing prolific letters to her friends.

Charlotte became pregnant shortly after her marriage to Arthur. Everyone was excited at the news of a new person, a little Bell to bring happiness to the home. Pregnancy was not easy for Charlotte, though. She was struck by severe morning sickness and couldn't hold down her food. She began losing

IN MEMORY OF
EMILY JANE BRONTË
WHO DIED DEC. 19TH 1848.
AGED 30 YEARS.
AND OF
CHARLOTTE BRONTË
BORN APRIL 21ST 1816
DIED MARCH 31ST 1855.

There is a memorial plaque over the crypt inside the floor of Haworth's St. Michael and all Angels church where Emily and Charlotte are buried.

weight, instead of gaining it. She became weak and frail and couldn't get out of bed.

The doctor was called, but nothing could be done to help her. Her father and husband worried about her, and the servants were miserable. On March 31, 1855, the church bell rang again to announce the death of another Brontë. Charlotte was only a few weeks away from her thirty-ninth birthday.

Although her death certificate claimed tuberculosis as the cause of death, contemporary medical opinion believes Charlotte's death was caused by excessive morning sickness. She simply couldn't hold down her food, and her body withered into dehydration and starvation.

Elizabeth Gaskell, Charlotte's dear friend and fellow author, wrote a biography of Charlotte at the request of Reverend Brontë. Mrs. Gaskell's book, *The Life of Charlotte Brontë*, was published in 1857 by Smith, Elder & Company. After it was published, people came from all over England to Haworth to see where the author had lived and written her books. Reverend Brontë lived another six years at the parsonage in Haworth with his son-in-law and curate, Arthur Bell Nicholls.

Hoping to honor his wife's literary legacy, Charlotte's husband edited her unpublished manuscript of *The Professor* and had it published with Smith, Elder & Company two years after her death.

Today, the parsonage at Haworth is a museum commemorating the Brontë sisters' lives and work. Visitors can see many of the sisters' clothing items, artwork, writing equipment, and hand-written materials. They can see where the three sisters wrote their visionary poems and novels and where

Glass Town and the kingdoms of Angria and Gondal had been imagined. Each year 85,000 people visit the Brontë Parsonage Museum in Haworth.

A bronze statue of the Brontë sisters by sculptor Jocelyn Horner stands in the garden outside the Bronte Parsonage Museum.

Charlotte Brontë

"I can be on guard against my enemies, but God deliver me from my friends!"
—Charlotte Brontë; letter to G. H. Lewes, November 6, 1847

"But life is a battle: may we all be enabled to fight it well!"
—Charlotte Brontë; letter to Ellen Nussey, September 24, 1849

"Gentle reader, may you never feel what I then felt! May your eyes never shed such stormy, scalding, heart-wrung tears as poured from mine. May you never appeal to Heaven in prayers so hopeless and so agonized as in that hour left my lips: for never may you, like me, dread to be the instrument of evil to what you wholly love."
—Charlotte Brontë; Jane Eyre, Chapter 27

"I'm just going to write because I cannot help it."
—Charlotte Brontë; Roe Head Journal fragment, October 1836

"I would always work in silence and obscurity, and let my efforts be known by their results."
—Charlotte Brontë; letter to Aunt Elizabeth Branwell, November 2, 1841

Emily Brontë

"A person who has not done one-half his day's work by ten o'clock, runs a chance of leaving the other half undone."
—Emily Brontë; Wuthering Heights, Chapter 7

"I'm wearying to escape into that glorious world, and to be always there; not seeing it dimly through tears, and yearning for it through the walls of an aching heart; but really with it, and in it."

—*Emily Brontë;* Wuthering Heights, *Chapter 15*

"No coward soul is mine
No trembler in the world's storm-troubled sphere
I see Heaven's glories shine
And Faith shines equal arming me from Fear"

— *Emily Brontë, "No Coward Soul Is Mine"*

Anne Brontë

"But smiles and tears are so alike with me, they are neither of them confined to any particular feelings: I often cry when I am happy, and smile when I am sad."

—*Anne Brontë;* The Tenant of Wildfell Hal*l, Chapter 15*

"It is foolish to wish for beauty. Sensible people never either desire it for themselves or care about it in others. If the mind be but well cultivated, and the heart well disposed, no one ever cares for the exterior."

—*Anne Brontë;* Agnes Grey, *Chapter 17*

£ = pounds sterling: A pound sterling, or simply referred to as a pound, is the monetary value of Great Britain; indicated with the symbol £

Anglo-Irish: Most commonly referring to people born in Ireland of English descent

Antibiotics: A substance that inhibits or kills a harmful microscopic creature, especially one that causes disease

Beck: A small stream or brook

Catechism: A summary of religious doctrine often in the form of questions and answers

Comportment: The bearing, behavior, or physical attitude of a person. Middle- and upper-class girls of previous ages were instructed how to walk, sit, speak, and behave like a lady

Conjecture: An opinion given without facts to back it up

Countenance: A person's face, facial appearance, and expressions

Coveted: Earnestly wished for or sought after

Crag: The face of a steep cliff, particularly with jagged pieces and projections of rock

Curate: A clergyman assigned to assist a higher level clergyman such as a vicar, rector, or priest

Devout: Committed or devoted to religion or to religious duties or exercises

Distempered: A person's behavior presenting frantic, hectic activity, as if uncontrollable

Entreat: A serious request of a person; to beg a person to do something on one's behalf

Frock: A woman's or girl's dress

Genies: Used here as a god-like creature who holds control over a location and all the people and animals that live there

Gentry: The upper or ruling class; landowners

Governess: A woman who teaches children at home

Heath: A type of shrubby, often-evergreen plants that grow well on poorly drained soil

Infuriate: To push a person into extreme anger or fury; something that brings a person to feel extreme anger or fury

Kirk: A church

Legacy: Used in this book to refer to money or property left to a person in a will; an inheritance

Melancholy: A feeling of sadness, doom, depression

Moors: A type of rocky landscape where little grows but heath, characterized by strong winds and harsh conditions

Nineteenth Century: The century of history that started in 1800 and ended with 1899

Parsonage: A house owned by the church where clergy and family reside

Pensionnat: French boarding school or academy

Pragmatic: An approach where reason and logic are applied; sensible

Precocious: Exhibiting mature qualities at an unusually early age

Prolific: The production of a great quantity of substance or material

Pseudonym: A false name used by people who don't want their real names known; a pen name

Royalties: Income earned by the accumulated sales of a product

Sexton: Caretaker of a church grounds, bell-ringer and/or gravedigger

Stationer: Publisher or bookseller

Textile: all manner of cloth, fabric, and ribbon of knit or woven material

Unscrupulous: Showing no regard for morals, duty or honor; without scruples

Vicar: A high-ranking member of the clergy responsible for a local church and assists with community matters

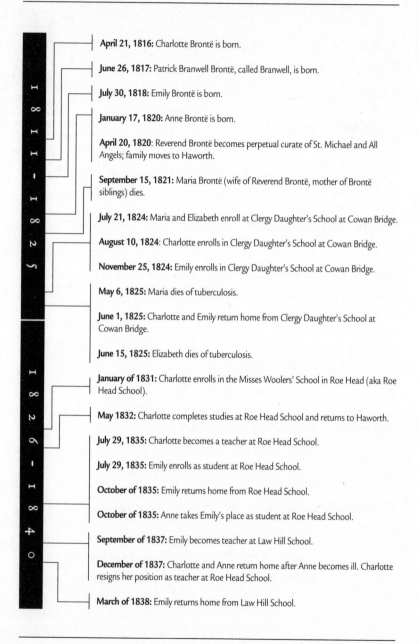

April 21, 1816: Charlotte Brontë is born.

June 26, 1817: Patrick Branwell Brontë, called Branwell, is born.

July 30, 1818: Emily Brontë is born.

January 17, 1820: Anne Brontë is born.

April 20, 1820: Reverend Brontë becomes perpetual curate of St. Michael and All Angels; family moves to Haworth.

September 15, 1821: Maria Brontë (wife of Reverend Brontë, mother of Brontë siblings) dies.

July 21, 1824: Maria and Elizabeth enroll at Clergy Daughter's School at Cowan Bridge.

August 10, 1824: Charlotte enrolls in Clergy Daughter's School at Cowan Bridge.

November 25, 1824: Emily enrolls in Clergy Daughter's School at Cowan Bridge.

May 6, 1825: Maria dies of tuberculosis.

June 1, 1825: Charlotte and Emily return home from Clergy Daughter's School at Cowan Bridge.

June 15, 1825: Elizabeth dies of tuberculosis.

January of 1831: Charlotte enrolls in the Misses Woolers' School in Roe Head (aka Roe Head School).

May 1832: Charlotte completes studies at Roe Head School and returns to Haworth.

July 29, 1835: Charlotte becomes a teacher at Roe Head School.

July 29, 1835: Emily enrolls as student at Roe Head School.

October of 1835: Emily returns home from Roe Head School.

October of 1835: Anne takes Emily's place as student at Roe Head School.

September of 1837: Emily becomes teacher at Law Hill School.

December of 1837: Charlotte and Anne return home after Anne becomes ill. Charlotte resigns her position as teacher at Roe Head School.

March of 1838: Emily returns home from Law Hill School.

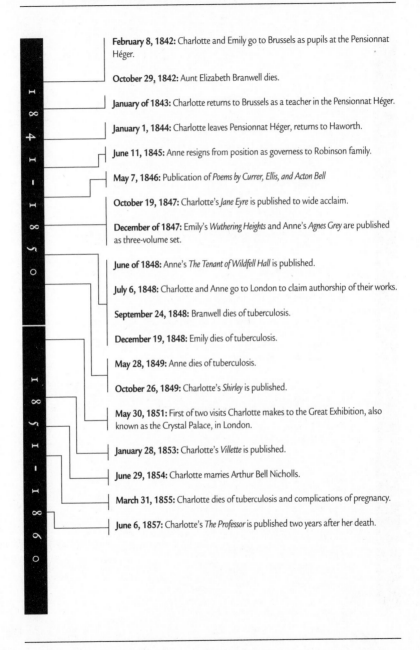

February 8, 1842: Charlotte and Emily go to Brussels as pupils at the Pensionnat Héger.

October 29, 1842: Aunt Elizabeth Branwell dies.

January of 1843: Charlotte returns to Brussels as a teacher in the Pensionnat Héger.

January 1, 1844: Charlotte leaves Pensionnat Héger, returns to Haworth.

June 11, 1845: Anne resigns from position as governess to Robinson family.

May 7, 1846: Publication of *Poems by Currer, Ellis, and Acton Bell*

October 19, 1847: Charlotte's *Jane Eyre* is published to wide acclaim.

December of 1847: Emily's *Wuthering Heights* and Anne's *Agnes Grey* are published as three-volume set.

June of 1848: Anne's *The Tenant of Wildfell Hall* is published.

July 6, 1848: Charlotte and Anne go to London to claim authorship of their works.

September 24, 1848: Branwell dies of tuberculosis.

December 19, 1848: Emily dies of tuberculosis.

May 28, 1849: Anne dies of tuberculosis.

October 26, 1849: Charlotte's *Shirley* is published.

May 30, 1851: First of two visits Charlotte makes to the Great Exhibition, also known as the Crystal Palace, in London.

January 28, 1853: Charlotte's *Villette* is published.

June 29, 1854: Charlotte marries Arthur Bell Nicholls.

March 31, 1855: Charlotte dies of tuberculosis and complications of pregnancy.

June 6, 1857: Charlotte's *The Professor* is published two years after her death.

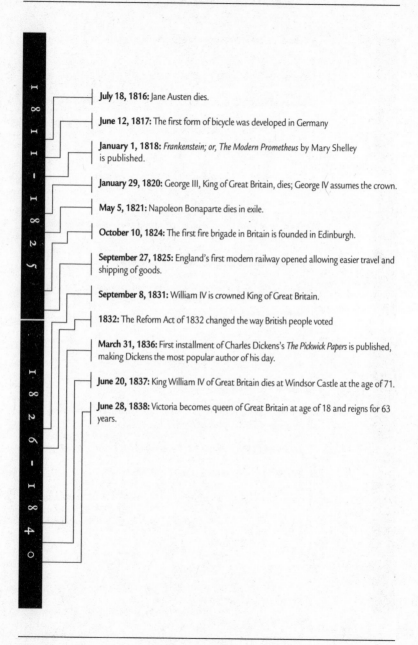

July 18, 1816: Jane Austen dies.

June 12, 1817: The first form of bicycle was developed in Germany

January 1, 1818: *Frankenstein; or, The Modern Prometheus* by Mary Shelley is published.

January 29, 1820: George III, King of Great Britain, dies; George IV assumes the crown.

May 5, 1821: Napoleon Bonaparte dies in exile.

October 10, 1824: The first fire brigade in Britain is founded in Edinburgh.

September 27, 1825: England's first modern railway opened allowing easier travel and shipping of goods.

September 8, 1831: William IV is crowned King of Great Britain.

1832: The Reform Act of 1832 changed the way British people voted

March 31, 1836: First installment of Charles Dickens's *The Pickwick Papers* is published, making Dickens the most popular author of his day.

June 20, 1837: King William IV of Great Britain dies at Windsor Castle at the age of 71.

June 28, 1838: Victoria becomes queen of Great Britain at age of 18 and reigns for 63 years.

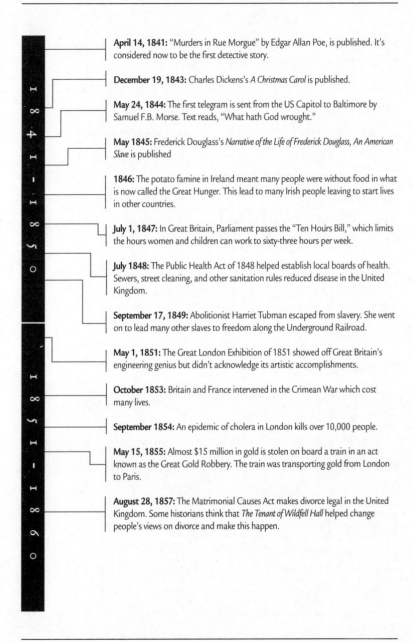

April 14, 1841: "Murders in Rue Morgue" by Edgar Allan Poe, is published. It's considered now to be the first detective story.

December 19, 1843: Charles Dickens's *A Christmas Carol* is published.

May 24, 1844: The first telegram is sent from the US Capitol to Baltimore by Samuel F.B. Morse. Text reads, "What hath God wrought."

May 1845: Frederick Douglass's *Narrative of the Life of Frederick Douglass, An American Slave* is published

1846: The potato famine in Ireland meant many people were without food in what is now called the Great Hunger. This lead to many Irish people leaving to start lives in other countries.

July 1, 1847: In Great Britain, Parliament passes the "Ten Hours Bill," which limits the hours women and children can work to sixty-three hours per week.

July 1848: The Public Health Act of 1848 helped establish local boards of health. Sewers, street cleaning, and other sanitation rules reduced disease in the United Kingdom.

September 17, 1849: Abolitionist Harriet Tubman escaped from slavery. She went on to lead many other slaves to freedom along the Underground Railroad.

May 1, 1851: The Great London Exhibition of 1851 showed off Great Britain's engineering genius but didn't acknowledge its artistic accomplishments.

October 1853: Britain and France intervened in the Crimean War which cost many lives.

September 1854: An epidemic of cholera in London kills over 10,000 people.

May 15, 1855: Almost $15 million in gold is stolen on board a train in an act known as the Great Gold Robbery. The train was transporting gold from London to Paris.

August 28, 1857: The Matrimonial Causes Act makes divorce legal in the United Kingdom. Some historians think that *The Tenant of Wildfell Hall* helped change people's views on divorce and make this happen.

Ellis, Samantha. 2017. *Take Courage: Anne Brontë and the Art of Life*. London: Chatto & Windus.

Fraser, Rebecca. 1988. *The Brontës: Charlotte Brontë and Her Family*. New York City: Crown.

Gaskell, Elizabeth. 1998. *The Life of Charlotte Brontë*. New York City: Penguin Classics.

Harman, Claire. 2016. *Charlotte Brontë: A Fiery Heart*. New York City: Knopf.

Lamonica, Drew. 2003. *We Are Three Sisters*. Columbia, Missouri: University of Missouri Press.

Lutz, Deborah. 2016. *The Brontë Cabinet*. New York City: W. W. Norton & Company.

Further Reading

Hubbart, Kate. 2004. *Who Was Charlotte Brontë*. London: Short Books Ltd.

Orme, David. 1999. *The Brontës*. London: Evans Brothers.

Pasachoff, Naomi. 2009. *A Student's Guide to the Brontë Sisters*. New York: Enslow Publishers.

Ross, Stewart. 1997. *Charlotte Brontë and Jane Eyre*. New York: Viking.

With a sword swallower as a father and a closet chanteuse for a mother, it's no wonder **Carolyn Burns Bass** became a writer. A longtime journalist for entertainment, travel and lifestyle media, Carolyn has blogged for the *Huffington Post* and about travel for Examiner.com. Her short fiction has been published in *The Rose & Thorn*, *Breath & Shadow*, and *MetroFiction* e-zines. As a finalist for the 2013 Eric Hoffer Award, her short story "Sketches Past and Present" appears in the anthology, *Best New Writing 2013*. Carolyn became a fan of the Brontë sisters when she first read *Wuthering Heights* in seventh grade. She went on to read *Jane Eyre* in high school and was finally introduced to the often-overlooked Anne when she read *The Tenant of Wildfell Hall* and *Agnes Grey* while in college. She has read *Wuthering Heights* from cover to cover too many times to count.

All About... Series

A series for inquisitive young readers

If you liked this book, you may also enjoy:

Also available as an audiobook!

All titles are available in print and ebook form!
Teachers guides and puzzles available at brpressbooks.com/all-about-teachers-guides/